HORSES

Isabel Orton

Grolier
an imprint of

www.scholastic.com/librarypublishing

Published 2009 by Grolier
An Imprint of Scholastic Library Publishing
Old Sherman Turnpike
Danbury, Connecticut 06816

For The Brown Reference Group plc
Project Editor: Jolyon Goddard
Picture Researchers: Clare Newman, Sophie
Mortimer
Designer: Sarah Williams
Managing Editor: Tim Harris

Volume ISBN-13: 978-0-7172-8046-9
Volume ISBN-10: 0-7172-8046-2

**Library of Congress
Cataloging-in-Publication Data**

Nature's children. Set 5.
   p. cm.
   Includes index.
   ISBN-13: 978-0-7172-8084-1
   ISBN-10: 0-7172-8084-5 (set)
   1. Animals--Encyclopedias, Juvenile. 1.
Grolier Educational (Firm)
   QL49.N386 2009
   590.3--dc22
                        2008014674

Printed and bound in China

PICTURE CREDITS

Front Cover: **Shutterstock**: Joe Gough.

Back Cover: **NaturePL**: Lynn M. Stone;
Shutterstock: Condor 36, Jeanne Hatch,
Abramova Kseniya.

Alamy: Picture Partners 18, Adrian Sherratt
26–27, tbkmedia.de 14, 37, 38; **Corbis**: The
Gallery Collection 9; **Shutterstock**: Eduard
Cebria 46, Karen Givens 29, Eric Isselee 4,
N. Joy Neish 10, Abramova Kseniya 5, 6, 41,
Holly Kuchera 33, Kondrashov Mikhail
Evgenevich 42, Sharon Morris 13, Sergey
Petrov 45, Kanwarjit Singh Boparai 34, Eline
Spek 21, Stockphotography 2–3, Thoma 30,
Diane Webb 17; **Still Pictures**: J. Klein and
M. Hubert 22.

Contents

FACT FILE: Horses

Class	Mammals (Mammalia)
Order	Odd-toed hoofed mammals (Perissodactyla)
Family	Horse family (Equidae)
Genus	Horses, zebras, and asses (*Equus*)
Species	Domesticated and feral horses (*Equus caballus*)
World distribution	Every continent except Antarctica
Habitat	Mostly grasslands
Distinctive physical characteristics	Wide variation in size and color, depending on breed
Habits	Like their wild ancestors, domestic horses prefer to live in small groups
Diet	Domesticated horses eat grass and are often also given hay, cereals, and commercially manufactured horse food

Introduction

For thousands of years, horses have helped people go places, work the land, and even ride into battle. Today, people ride and drive horses mostly for sport and pleasure. There are many different types of horses. Some are huge and powerful, with the strength to pull heavy loads. Others are built for racing. Most horses are gentle, and willing to do what people ask them—from jumping over a fence to rounding up cattle.

Horses were domesticated later than other animals, such as cattle and dogs.

Horses can run very fast.
They use speed to escape
their enemies.

Large and Small

There are more than 100 different **breeds** of horses. Horses come in all sizes from huge shire horses to sleek racehorses and sturdy Shetland ponies. Horses come in many colors, too. The most common colors include black, brown, chestnut, and gray. Many horses have white markings on their face and legs. Some horses have unusual colors, such as paint or pinto horses. Their coats have a bold pattern of white and either black or brown patches. Appaloosas (A-PUH-LOO-SUHZ) have a white coat covered in black spots. Palominos (PA-LUH-MEE-NOZE) are cream or golden, with a white mane and tail.

A horse's height is measured from the ground to the top of the shoulders in units called **hands**. One hand equals 4 inches (10 cm) and is about the width of an adult person's hand. Small horses standing no taller than 14½ hands (1.5 m) are called ponies. The biggest horses may be more than 18 hands (1.8 m) tall.

People and Horses

People and horses have been together for tens of thousands of years. Paintings of horses from about 30,000 years ago have been found on cave walls. Back then, horses were probably hunted for their meat.

No one really knows for sure how long ago horses were first **domesticated**. Remains of horses and war chariots have been found at grave sites in Central Asia dating back 6,000 years. In fact, one of the most important uses for horses in the ancient world was in warfare. Sculptures and paintings from the great civilizations of the past, such as in Greece and Egypt, often show warriors riding or driving horses.

Domesticated horses first arrived in the United States with the Spanish explorers of the 1500s. By that time, horses had been used for hundreds of years all over Europe. Native Americans became expert horse riders. They used their horses for hunting and in battle.

This picture of a horse, surrounded by arrows, was painted on a cave wall thousands of years ago.

9

Pulling a plow is hard work, so draft horses are often driven in teams to share the task.

Workhorses

How did people get around before the invention of automobiles? Horsepower! Horses were used to pull carts and carriages and to take people from place to place. For long-distance trips, covered wagons and stage coaches carrying passengers or mail were pulled by teams of as many as four or six horses. Many people kept their own horses and wagons for traveling.

Horses were used for farmwork, too. They pulled plows that farmers used to work the land. Those farm horses, known as **draft horses**, were often very large and powerfully built. They originally came over from Europe with early settlers. Draft horses included the enormous, shaggy-legged Clydesdales from Scotland and sturdy Suffolk horses from eastern England. Other big work horses included the Percheron (PUR-SHUH-RON) from France. Draft horses are still seen in the United States today. But these days, tractors and other machines are used in farming. People mostly keep draft horses for displays and shows.

Back to Nature

Horses were tamed by people long ago. But they have not lost all their natural ways. They still sometimes behave as they would in the wild.

By nature, horses live in groups called **bands**. In a wild band, there are always horses that have a higher rank than others. They have first pick of any food and decide where the band goes. Horses that have a lower rank might have to stay on the outskirts of the band or wait their turn to feed.

Domesticated horses behave in the same way. Most of them get along well together. But when several horses share a field, there is nearly always one that tries to boss the others around. There might be kicking and jostling over food. The more timid animals may get pushed aside.

Horses have also kept their natural instinct to run away from anything that frightens them. They are easily startled by strange noises and objects. People who keep horses learn to handle them gently and quietly.

A pair of horses shows their friendship by nibbling each other's neck and mane.

Stabled horses like to have a door to look over, so that they can see people or other horses.

14

Horses at Home

A building for a horse to live in is called a stable. Some people keep their horses in a stable all year round, and allow them out into a field only for occasional exercise. Other horse owners keep their horses out at pasture and just bring them inside at night or in winter. Inside or outdoors, a horse must be safe and comfortable.

A stable should have plenty of fresh air. It must also provide enough room for a horse to turn around or lie down. The floor can be either dirt or concrete. It should be covered with matting or material such as straw or wood shavings to provide a soft bed. Wet or dirty bedding must be removed and replaced every day. The horse needs a bucket of clean drinking water at all times.

Every pasture or **corral** should have some form of shelter, where a horse can get away from the hot sun or heavy rain. Unless there is a natural water source, such as a stream, a water trough is essential. Horse owners should check their pasture regularly for anything harmful, such as plants that could poison a horse.

The Right Food

The natural diet for horses is grass. Grass contains the **fiber** that their stomach is designed to break down, or digest. Grass is low in nutrients, so horses in the wild spend much of their time grazing to get enough energy from their food. Domesticated horses can survive on grass, too. But if they are ridden regularly and working hard, they need extra energy-giving food to stay fit.

Many people add cereals such as oats to their horses' diet. These cereals provide energy very quickly. However, such foods sometimes give horses so much energy that they are difficult to ride! There are many different types of prepared horse foods available that contain a mixture of high-energy food and fiber. Those foods help provide domesticated horses with a balanced diet.

Horses that are kept in stables most of the time also need a daily supply of dry grass, or hay. That allows them to eat throughout the day, as they would do naturally in the wild.

Chewing hay produces saliva in a horse's mouth. Saliva helps the horse digest its food properly.

17

A grooming
session is a good
time to check
a horse or pony
for any small
cuts or other
minor injuries.

Grooming

Brushing and cleaning a horse's coat is called grooming. Grooming makes horses look nice and helps them stay healthy, too. Regular brushing keeps the coat in good condition. It also **tones up** a horse's muscles.

A person who tends horses is known as a groom. He or she usually starts by cleaning the horse's legs, using a stiff-bristled brush, called a dandy brush, to remove mud. A horse left with muddy legs might develop skin **infections** that take a long time to heal. The groom uses a softer brush to clean a horse's body. The groom makes long sweeps across the coat to remove any dirt, dried sweat, and flakes of skin. It is very important to brush any areas that lie under a **saddle** or **bridle**. If dirt is trapped beneath the leather straps, it rubs the skin and can cause sore areas. Either a soft brush or a wide-toothed comb is used to get the tangles out of a mane and tail. Finally, dirt or stones that have become stuck underneath the hooves are removed with a tool called a hoofpick.

Tack

Saddles and bridles are known as **tack**. Bridles have a metal bar, called a bit, which rests in the horse's mouth. A rider puts gentle pressure on the bit through reins attached to each end of the bar. By pulling tight or loose on the reins, a rider gives the horse instructions. A well-trained horse knows by the feel of the reins when the rider wants to slow down, stop, or change direction. Good riders never use the reins alone to control their horses. They use their legs and body as well.

The saddle is fastened by a strap, called a girth, that passes under the horse's belly. Together with the **stirrups**, the saddle allows the rider to sit in a secure position. Saddles also help keep a rider on the part of the horse's back that is best able to bear weight. A saddle placed too far forward or too far back is very uncomfortable for a horse.

The metal bit of a bridle rests comfortably at the back of a horse's mouth, where there are no teeth.

bridle

bit

rein

A Navajo girl from Arizona has her first riding lesson.

In the Saddle

Learning to ride a horse well takes many years. The best way to learn is to be taught by an experienced instructor. For safety, many people first learn in a small field or an indoor school.

The first thing any new rider needs to know is how to get on the horse! The rider stands on the left-hand, or near, side of the horse, facing the tail, and places a foot in the stirrup. Then, holding the saddle, the rider swings up, turns around, and sits down as lightly as possible. Standing on a wooden or stone block or having someone boost the rider onto the horse makes getting into the saddle much easier.

Once in the saddle, a rider learns how to control the horse in all the ways it moves. The different ways a horse moves are called **gaits**. They include walking, trotting, a gentle, loping gait called cantering, and galloping. By making slight movements of the legs, a rider asks the horse to change pace or direction. At the same time, the rider also uses the reins, without pulling or tugging, to help steer the horse.

Riding Out

A horse that lives in a field most of the time usually gets plenty of exercise. A horse that is always in a stable needs to be ridden more often than one that lives outside. Being full of excess energy can easily make a horse difficult to manage. And, as with humans, lack of exercise affects a horse's fitness.

Horses usually enjoy being out and about, especially if they are with other horses. Being ridden along tracks and trails, or in open country, gives them new things to look at. That helps keep them alert and interested in life. Like humans, horses can easily become bored and that might affect their general well-being.

The right amount of riding gives horses healthy exercise without overstraining them. A good rider always starts off at an easy pace to allow the horse to warm up. A rider should go home slowly so that the horse relaxes and cools down.

Western Style

A popular type of riding in the United States is the Western style. It's the way cowboys and cowgirls in the American West ride. Western style is still seen on some working ranches. But most people today ride that way just for pleasure or in shows or rodeos.

In Western riding, the rider holds the reins in one hand and controls the horse mainly by the pressure of the reins on its neck. That is how riders can keep one hand free to use a **lasso** for roping cattle. Neck-reining, as it is called, also means that Western riders can change direction easily as they follow the twists and turns of fast-moving cattle herds.

The saddles used for Western riding have a deep seat and long stirrups. That allows the rider to sink down comfortably and stay balanced, even when riding over rough ground. At the front of the saddle there is a knob, called a horn. Once a rider has lassoed a cow or bull, he or she keeps hold of it by winding the end of the lasso around the horn.

These riders are wearing safety helmets. A helmet helps protect the head if a rider falls off or bumps into the branch of a tree.

Mares and Stallions

Horses can **mate** at any time of the year. Female horses, or **mares**, are old enough to breed when they are about three years old. Male horses, or **stallions**, are usually ready to breed at a younger age. Stallions are often highly spirited animals. Some of them are difficult to handle. That is why many male horses are neutered, or gelded, which means that they cannot be used for breeding. They are called **geldings** and tend to be calmer than stallions.

A mare is pregnant for about 11 or 12 months. She should only exercise lightly during that time. She may also need special food to keep her fit and healthy.

A frisky white Arabian stallion runs around in its field. Its nostrils expand, or flare, to take in as much air as possible.

A foal stays with its mother for the first few months of its life. Most foals stop nursing before they are one year old.

Soon on Their Feet

Most mares give birth to just one baby, or **foal**. Sometimes twins are born, but they are rare. A male foal is called a **colt** and a female foal is called a **filly**.

Almost as soon as a foal is born, it staggers to its feet and starts nursing, or drinking, its mother's milk. Within a few hours, the foal can gallop and kick up its heels in play. Such rapid progress is nature's way of giving foals the best chance of survival. In the wild, foals have to be able to flee from danger as soon after birth as possible.

Newborn foals have a soft, sometimes woolly, coat. Their tail, instead of being long and flowing like that of an adult horse, is short and curly. Foals grow quickly and their color often changes as they get older. For example, gray horses are always born black. They turn paler as they grow up.

Good Behavior

Teaching a young horse how to behave well and carry a rider safely takes time and patience. A horse must not be frightened during its training, or allowed to misbehave. It might learn bad habits that can last a lifetime.

Lessons begin early in a foal's life. Horse trainers often start by just grooming a foal very gently. Foals usually enjoy that, and they soon learn to stand quietly while they are being handled. Next, they learn to wear a **halter** for a few minutes at a time. They soon become used to being led around and tied up.

Most horses are not strong enough to be ridden until they are at least three years old. Then their real training begins. First, a young horse is taught to wear a saddle and bridle. The trainer does not ride the horse at this stage. The trainer guides it through exercises such as turning and stopping. In time, the horse accepts the weight of a rider on its back.

This foal has become used to wearing a halter made of soft webbing.

The Kentucky Derby
is a famous horse race
in the United States.

Thoroughbreds

Thoroughbreds are among the most beautiful and valuable horses in the world. A special breed, they are long-legged horses that are both slender and strong. They are used for riding, but they are most famous for being very fast racehorses. At top speed, a thoroughbred racehorse can gallop at about 45 miles (72 km) an hour. No other breed of horse can match that speed.

When thoroughbreds are used for racing, they start their training much earlier than most other horses do. Because they are strong and also because they are given special food, they grow up very quickly. Thoroughbreds often run in their first race when they are only two years old. Their riders, or jockeys, are very lightweight, so the young horses can carry them easily.

All thoroughbreds share the same three Arabian stallions as distant ancestors. The stallions were brought to England from Hungary, Syria, and Tunisia in the late 1600s and early 1700s. They were used to breed fast horses.

Quarter Horses

One of the best-loved breeds of horses in the United States is the American quarter horse. This horse was first bred in the 1600s by settlers in southern states such as Virginia and South Carolina. Quarter horses were given their name because they were originally kept for running short races over tracks of one-quarter mile (0.4 km). When they were not racing, they were also used for general riding or for pulling light carts.

Quarter horses cannot compete with thoroughbred racehorses or race over long distances. But they are amazing sprinters. Their very powerful hindquarters enable them to make a quick start and have tremendous bursts of speed.

Today, quarter horses are popular as saddle horses. They are often kept on ranches, where modern ranchers still sometimes ride them to round up cattle. The horses' speed and ability to turn swiftly make them perfectly suited to their work.

The American quarter horse is popular with people who like to ride Western style.

37

The speed of a Tennessee walking horse's "running walk" might be up to 10 miles (16 km) per hour.

Fast Walkers

In the early 1800s, the farmers of Tennessee produced a type of horse that could carry them easily over their vast lands. This horse is now known as the Tennessee walking horse. The horse became famous both for its endurance and its special gait. Walking horses walk, trot, and canter in the same way as other horses. But they have another gait, too. They can move at a fast walk that is almost like running, but much smoother. This gliding gait carries the walking horse easily over great distances. It also means that a rider can sit comfortably in the saddle all day.

Walking horses are very popular at shows and are amazing to watch in action. They are sometimes trained to lift their front legs and front part of their body very high. That makes them look as though they are almost sitting on their tail!

Competition

Show jumping is very popular, both with riders and spectators. Competitions for riders of all abilities are held in any country where horses are ridden for sport.

In a competition, a rider follows a set course of jumps. Those may include poles, gates, hedges, walls, and water-filled ditches. The aim of the rider and horse is to jump a clear round. That means completing the course without knocking anything down. Penalty points are given if a horse knocks down part of an obstacle or refuses to jump it. If several riders jump clear, they enter more rounds to decide the winner. In some competitions, the jumps in the second round are made higher. In others, the riders are timed and the fastest to jump a clear round wins.

Show jumpers, both horse and rider, must be bold and have a good eye for judging the distances between jumps. The best competitors go through many years of hard training.

The white bandages around this show jumping horse's legs give support and help prevent injury through strains.

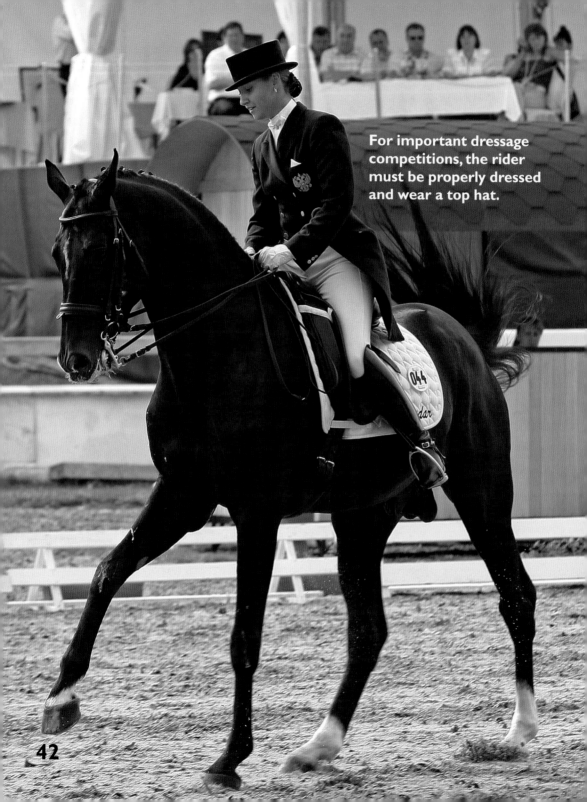

For important dressage competitions, the rider must be properly dressed and wear a top hat.

Dressage

Some riders train their horses to perform special exercises, called dressage (DREH-SARZH). In dressage, a horse has to change pace exactly as its rider asks and make movements sideways, diagonally, or even backward! Practicing the exercises helps make a horse **agile** and obedient.

Dressage competitions are often held at horse shows. They are performed in an arena, which is marked at various points with letters of the alphabet. The rider must learn a test in which the horse has to make certain movements between one letter and another. For example, the horse and rider may be asked to trot around the arena from B to E, or make a circle starting at K. If the rider forgets the test and goes in the wrong direction, he or she is given penalty points. Penalties are also given if the horse goes at the wrong pace or does not move smoothly. It takes a skilled rider to perform a good test.

Fast-paced Polo

One of the most exciting horse sports is the game of polo. The sport is played on a large field or in an indoor arena. There are two teams of riders—four on each team for outdoor polo and three on each team for indoor polo. They use long mallets to hit a ball through goalposts at either end of the field. The pace is fast as the teams race to reach the ball. A match is divided into four periods called chukkers. Because polo is such a fast and furious game, the riders change their horses after every chukker. The horses used in polo are always called "ponies," whatever their size.

Polo probably was first played more than 4,000 years ago in Persia—now called Iran. It spread to India and became a sport of the mogul (MO-GUL) emperors. In the 1800s, British people living in India took up polo and helped make the game popular around the world.

Polo players have to keep an eye on the ball and control their ponies at the same time.

For each stride, a trotting horse lifts the front leg and back leg on the opposite sides at the same time.

Harness Racing

The sport of **harness** racing is also popular in the United States. In harness racing, horses run pulling light, two-wheeled carts known as sulkies. The driver balances on a small seat.

The type of horses used in harness racing is called standardbreds. They do not gallop like other racehorses but use two types of gaits called trotting and pacing. A trotter moves diagonally. That means that the horse lifts its right front leg and left back leg at the same time, and then the left front leg and the right back leg. A pacer moves by lifting front and back legs together on the same side. At either gait, the horses can travel very fast. Trotters and pacers are trained in different ways and take part in separate races.

Harness races take place on oval tracks. They cover a distance of 1 mile (1.6 km). If a horse changes its gait to a canter or gallop, it is disqualified.

Special Care

Domestic horses rely on people for all their daily needs. From time to time, they need special care and attention.

Some of the most important people who take care of horses are blacksmiths. They are experts in caring for a horse's feet and fitting the metal shoes worn by all working horses. The shoes wear down quickly and often also become loose. Every few weeks, a good owner takes his or her horse to the blacksmith to have the shoes replaced. The blacksmith also trims the hooves, which grow all the time, like fingernails and toenails.

Sometimes horses get sick. They might injure a leg, or go lame, and cannot move properly. They might also have coughs and colds or digestive problems. Then, it is time to call in a veterinarian, or animal doctor, who will examine the horse and recommend treatment.

Horses are wonderful animals that work willingly for people and give a lot of pleasure. Taking care of them is a big commitment—but they deserve the best!

Words to Know

Agile Able to move easily, quickly, and gracefully.

Bands Groups of wild horses.

Breeds Types or varieties; to produce young.

Bridle The headgear worn by a ridden horse. It includes straps, the bit, and the reins.

Colt A male horse less than three years old.

Corral A pen or enclosure for animals.

Domesticated Bred and raised by humans.

Draft horses Strong horses used for pulling heavy carts or farm equipment.

Fiber Tough matter in plants.

Filly A female horse under three years of age.

Foal A baby horse.

Gaits The leg movements used by a horse to move at different speeds.

Geldings	Neutered male horses.
Halter	Strips of leather, webbing, or rope worn on a horse's head to enable it to be led around.
Hands	Unit of measurement of horses. One hand is equal to 4 inches (10 cm).
Harness	Equipment worn by a horse that pulls a cart or carriage.
Infections	Illnesses caused by germs.
Lasso	A rope with a loop at one end, used for catching cattle.
Mares	Adult female horses.
Mate	To come together to produce young.
Saddle	A rider's seat. Saddles are usually padded and covered in leather.
Stallions	Adult male horses.
Stirrups	Metal hoops hung on straps from a saddle to support a rider's feet.
Tack	Saddles and bridles.
Tones up	Keeps (the muscles) strong and in good working order.

Find Out More

Books

Horse. Eyewitness Books. New York: Dorling Kindersley, 2004.

Wagner, K. and S. Racine. *The Everything Kids' Horses Book: Hours of Off-the-hoof Fun!* Cincinnati, Ohio: Adams Media Corporation, 2006.

Web sites

Horse
www.enchantedlearning.com/subjects/mammals/horse/Horsecoloring.shtml
Facts about horses and a diagram to print and color in.

Horsefun
horsefun.com/
Information about horses and horse-related games to play.

Index